Cinco de Mayo

Crabtree Publishing Company

www.crabtreebooks.com

Crabtree Publishing Company

www.crabtreebooks.com

Author: Kate Torpie
Coordinating editor: Chester Fisher
Series editor: Susan Labella
Project manager: Kavita Lad (Q2AMEDIA)
Art direction: Dibakar Acharjee (Q2AMEDIA)
Cover design: Tarang Saggar (Q2AMEDIA)
Design: Neha Gupta (Q2AMEDIA)
Photo research: Anju Pathak (Q2AMEDIA)
Editor: Kelley MacAulay
Copy editor: Adrianna Morganelli
Proofreaders: Crystal Sikkens, Ken Wright
Project coordinator: Robert Walker
Production coordinator: Katherine Kantor
Font management: Mike Golka
Prepress technicians: Katherine Kantor, Ken Wright

Photographs:
Cover: Obi Juan Kenobi/Flickr; Odm/Dreamstime
(background); Title page: Jeremy Woodhouse/Jupiter
Images; P4: Odm/Dreamstime; P5: Tim Boyle/Staff/ Getty
Images; P6: Library of Congress Prints and Photographs;
P7: The London Art Archive/Alamy; P8: John Lund/Sam
Diephuis/Jupiter Images; P11: Jon Arnold Images Ltd/
Alamy; P12: Polka Dot Images/Jupiter Images; P13:
Joegough/Dreamstime; P14: Alexis Rodriguez-Duarte/
Jupiter Images; P15: Steve Vidler/Jupiter Images; P17:
Visions of America, LLC/Alamy; P19: Chris Curtis/
Shutterstock; P20: ClassicStock/Alamy; P21: Al Grillo/
Associated Press; P22: Robert Fried/Alamy; P23: Glenjones/
Dreamstime (dog); P23: Kittisuper/BigStockPhoto (crown);
P24: Ismael Rojas/Associated Press; P25: Eduardo Verdugo/
Associated Press; P26: Grady Harrison/Alamy; P28:
Antonio Iacovelli/Shutterstock (top); P28: Afronova/
Shutterstock (centre); P28: Geoff Kuchera/Istockphoto
(bottom); P29: Matthew Mawson/Alamy; P30:
Fozrocket/BigStockPhoto; P31: Robert Fried/Alamy

Illustrations:
Q2A Media Art Bank: P27

Library and Archives Canada Cataloguing in Publication

Torpie, Kate, 1974-
    Cinco de Mayo / Kate Torpie.

(Celebrations in my world)
Includes index.
ISBN 978-0-7787-4281-4 (bound).--ISBN 978-0-7787-4299-9 (pbk.)

    1. Cinco de Mayo (Mexican holiday)--Juvenile literature. I. Title.
II. Series.

F1233.T67 2008   j394.262   C2008-904105-4

Library of Congress Cataloging-in-Publication Data

Torpie, Kate, 1974-
  Cinco de mayo / Kate Torpie.
      p. cm. -- (Celebrations in my world)
  Includes index.
  ISBN-13: 978-0-7787-4299-9 (pbk. : alk. paper)
  ISBN-10: 0-7787-4299-7 (pbk. : alk. paper)
  ISBN-13: 978-0-7787-4281-4 (reinforced library binding : alk. paper)
  ISBN-10: 0-7787-4281-4 (reinforced library binding : alk. paper)
    1. Cinco de Mayo (Mexican holiday)--Juvenile literature. 2. Mexico--Social
life and customs--Juvenile literature. 3. Cinco de Mayo, Battle of, Puebla,
Mexico, 1862--Juvenile literature. I. Title.
    F1233.T644 2009
    394.262--dc22
                                                        2008028866

Crabtree Publishing Company

www.crabtreebooks.com   1-800-387-7650

Published in Canada
Crabtree Publishing
616 Welland Ave.
St. Catharines, ON
L2M 5V6

Published in the United States
Crabtree Publishing
PMB16A
350 Fifth Ave., Suite 3308
New York, NY 10118

Published in the United Kingdom
Crabtree Publishing
White Cross Mills
High Town, Lancaster
LA1 4XS

Published in Australia
Crabtree Publishing
386 Mt. Alexander Rd.
Ascot Vale (Melbourne)
VIC 3032

Contents

Cinco de Mayo **4**

How Did It Begin? **6**

Getting Ready! **8**

Street Fairs **10**

Fiesta Food **12**

Fiesta Costumes **14**

Fiesta Music **16**

What a Parade! **18**

The Jaribe Tapatio **20**

Fiestas Abroad **22**

Fiestas in Mexico **24**

Made in Mexico **26**

Mexican Art **28**

Viva Mexico! **30**

Glossary and Index **32**

Cinco de Mayo

Happy **Cinco de Mayo**! Cinco de Mayo is Spanish for May 5th. On this date, Mexican culture is celebrated. On *Cinco de Mayo*, everyone gets to be Mexican for a day!

● This is the flag of Mexico. Expect to see many flags waving on Cinco de Mayo!

DID. YOU KNOW?

The first Cinco de Mayo *was in California—not Mexico!*

Across the United States and Mexico, many *fiestas*, the Spanish word for parties, take place in honor of *Cinco de Mayo*. A *fiesta* includes wonderful Mexican food, music, and dancing!

How Did It Begin?

Do you know why *Cinco de Mayo* is celebrated on May 5th? Mexico no longer wanted to be a French colony. They wanted independence. They gained independence on May 5, 1862. On this day, Mexico won an important battle against France.

- A colonel named Porfirio Diaz helped Mexico win the battle on May 5, 1862. Later he became president of Mexico.

DID YOU KNOW?

Although Cinco de Mayo *celebrates this battle, many people today still believe that* Cinco de Mayo *celebrates the day Mexico won its independence.*

The Mexican army was outnumbered, but the colonel was clever! He freed a huge herd of cattle. They ran in different directions and confused the French army. The trick helped Mexico win the battle.

Getting Ready!

To prepare for *Cinco de Mayo*, people decorate homes and businesses. *Fiestas* are planned with Mexican games and crafts. Many people make **piñatas**. A *piñata* is a container filled with candy. Use the directions on the next page to make your own *piñata*!

A *piñata* makes a fun game. People wear blindfolds and hit the *piñata* with sticks. When the *piñata* breaks, candy spills out everywhere!

How to Make an Easy *Piñata*

1. Blow up a big balloon.

2. Mix 2 cups of flour and 3 cups of water together until it becomes a thick paste.

3. Tear a newspaper into strips. Dip the strips into the mixture.

4. Cover the balloon with the wet strips. Wait for them to dry.

5. Once the strips have dried, paint or sprinkle glitter over them.

6. Pop the balloon.

7. Cut a small hole at the top of the *piñata*. Fill it with candy.

8. Hang the *piñata* and start swinging!

DID YOU KNOW?

Piñatas *were once made from a clay-based pottery.* Piñatas *are made in the shape of animals, toys, or fruit.*

Street Fairs

After decorating their homes, many Mexican people head out to enjoy a street fair. Each town has its own *Zocalo*, or town square, where the fair takes place. During a street fair, the square hosts a lively celebration filled with music and bright colors. Vendors sell food in stalls on nearby streets. Restaurants offer traditional Mexican foods. People watch shows that include Mexican dancing and music.

DID YOU KNOW?

Sometimes musicians hold their concerts in the Zocalo.

Everyone has fun making noise with whistles, rattles, and horns. Children love taking part in the games and rides that are part of most street fairs.

The *Zocalo* in Mexico City is one of the largest squares in the world.

Fiesta Food

No *fiesta* is complete without food—and Mexican food is celebrated on *Cinco de Mayo! Tortillas* are part of many Mexican meals. Kids can help roll them up into sandwiches, or fry them with cheese to make *quesadillas.* Other Mexican foods include *salsa* and *tamales.*

● Kids roll *tortillas* into sandwiches or fry them with cheese to make *quesadillas.*

DID YOU KNOW?

Mole Poblano *is the national dish of Mexico. It's a bit firey, but also a bit sweet—it's made with chocolate!* Mole Poblano *uses chicken or turkey. What a sweet deal!*

Quick and Easy *Tacos*

Try this recipe at home. Be sure to have an adult help you.

1. You will need *taco* shells, tomatoes, lettuce, cheddar cheese, and one pound of ground chicken, beef, or turkey. You will also need *taco* seasoning. You may want sour cream for flavor.

2. Cook the meat until it is brown. When it is cooked, pour out the oil. Add one cup of water and a packet of *taco* seasoning. Let it simmer on low for five minutes.

3. Cut the lettuce and tomatoes into small pieces.

4. Shred the cheese.

5. Warm the *taco* shells in the microwave for 30 seconds.

6. Fill up your *taco* any way you like! Hint: put the cheese under the meat— the heat will make the cheese melt!

Fiesta Costumes

As if eating all those good foods wasn't enough fun, you also get to dress up for *Cinco de Mayo*! Mexican families may dress in traditional clothing in red, green, or white.

These people celebrate their Mexican heritage, or background, by wearing traditional clothes as they dance.

A man's traditional costume is called a **charro**. It includes a Mexican hat called a **sombrero**, and a bright, sparkly jacket. Ladies may wear skirts with ruffles that fluff out during dancing. Their shawls are knit in a Mexican style.

Children celebrate their Mexican heritage by wearing traditional clothes.

DID YOU KNOW?

The word charro *comes from the Mexican word for horseman.*

Fiesta Music

What else do you need for a *Cinco de Mayo fiesta*? Mexican music! Everyone at a *fiesta* or street fair gets excited when they hear the **Mariachi** band coming. The word *mariachi* once meant to dance on a wooden stage. Today, it is the name of a kind of music. *Mariachi* bands often have four to ten members. They are well known for the traditional Mexican folk music that they sing and play.

DID YOU KNOW?

The title of the song "La Cucuracha" means "The Cockroach." Some say the song is about a Mexican general's old carriage. Like a cockroach, it was dirty and ugly.

These bands also play modern music such as mambo or cha-cha songs. The dance songs are usually fast and lively, and have strong rhythms. Band members play instruments such as violins, trumpets, and guitars. *Mariachi* bands often play their music at celebrations, dances, and even schools.

Mariachi bands may play on stage, but not always! Sometimes, they stroll through a crowd. When they get close, crowds dance along with their music.

17

What a Parade!

Parades are a popular part of *Cinco de Mayo* celebrations. Many people get up very early to find a good spot along the street to watch the parade. Music is an important part of these parades, and school bands are excited to participate. School marching bands practice and rehearse their music for months so they can perform and compete against other bands.

DID YOU KNOW?

Some Cinco de Mayo *parade floats show people or events from Mexico's history.*

Look at this skirt swirling!
This lucky girl is performing
in a *Cinco de Mayo* parade!

The Jaribe Tapatio

A very popular Mexican dance is called the **Jaribe Tapatio**. That translates into "Hat Dance." *Jaribe Tapatio* isn't just a dance, it's also a game. And it isn't easy!

Children love to take part in Mexican dances.

At the end of a lively dance, these happy children are exhausted!

How to Dance the *Jaribe Tapatio*

You will need a hat and the right song!
An adult can help you find it, or sing it for you.
The beat of the song is 1, 2, 3, and 4!
On the "and 4" beat, clap twice and yell, "Ole!"

Step 1: Put a hat on the ground.
Greet your partner across the hat.
Boys bow and girls curtsy.

Step 2: Girls, hold onto your skirts; boys,
fold your arms behind your backs.

Step 3: Dance circles around the hat to the beat.
Don't forget to clap and yell, "Ole!"

Step 4: Try to keep up as the music gets faster.
Don't step on the hat!

Fiestas Abroad

Cinco de Mayo is a holiday to celebrate the history and culture of Mexico. Olvera Street in Los Angeles, California, has a large Mexican population. This wonderful community carries out many of Mexico's cultural traditions, including *Cinco de Mayo* festivities. People celebrate with parades, Mexican folk music and dance, and *piñata* games. There is also storytelling of the heroes and history of Mexico.

● Wow! This community has a parade to show off its pride. That's some *fiesta*!

In Arizona, the Chihuahua, a dog from Mexico, is honored on *Cinco de Mayo*. There is a Chihuahua parade—and one lucky pair of Chihuahuas is voted the king and queen of the day!

This dog is a Chihuahua winner!

DID YOU KNOW?

Low riders cars are often part of Cinco de Mayo *parades. Their owners fix up these old cars to look beautiful. The owners drive them in the parades.*

23

Fiestas in Mexico

The Mexican army won a battle on May 5th. That battle took place in the town of Puebla, and its people throw a very special *fiesta* on *Cinco de Mayo*. Soldiers march in a large parade to say thank you to all the people who gave their lives while fighting in Puebla. Army tanks and other vehicles follow them.

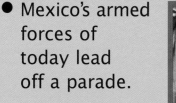

- Mexico's armed forces of today lead off a parade.

Music and food such as *tacos*, snow cones, and lemonade are also a large part of this town's festivities.

In Penon, Mexico, a different performance happens. People dress like the Mexican and French armies did in 1862. They act out the battle of long ago.

DID YOU KNOW?

In Penon, people begin planning for the next Cinco de Mayo on May 6th— a whole year ahead of time.

Made in Mexico

Cinco de Mayo is a lot of fun, but it's also an important day. It gives us a chance to learn about the rich Mexican history. It teaches us about the brave Mexican army that defeated the French and helped Mexicans come together for their country. Today, the battlefield is a park. The Mexican fort is a museum. Inside the museum, toy soldiers are set up to show what happened on May 5th, 1862.

General Zaragosa led the Mexican army to defeat the French. His statue honors him in Puebla today.

MEXICANOS:
LOS HIJOS DE ESTA GENERACION
NACIMOS LIBRES
ASI NOS CONSERVAREMOS
O MORIREMOS EN LA DEMANDA

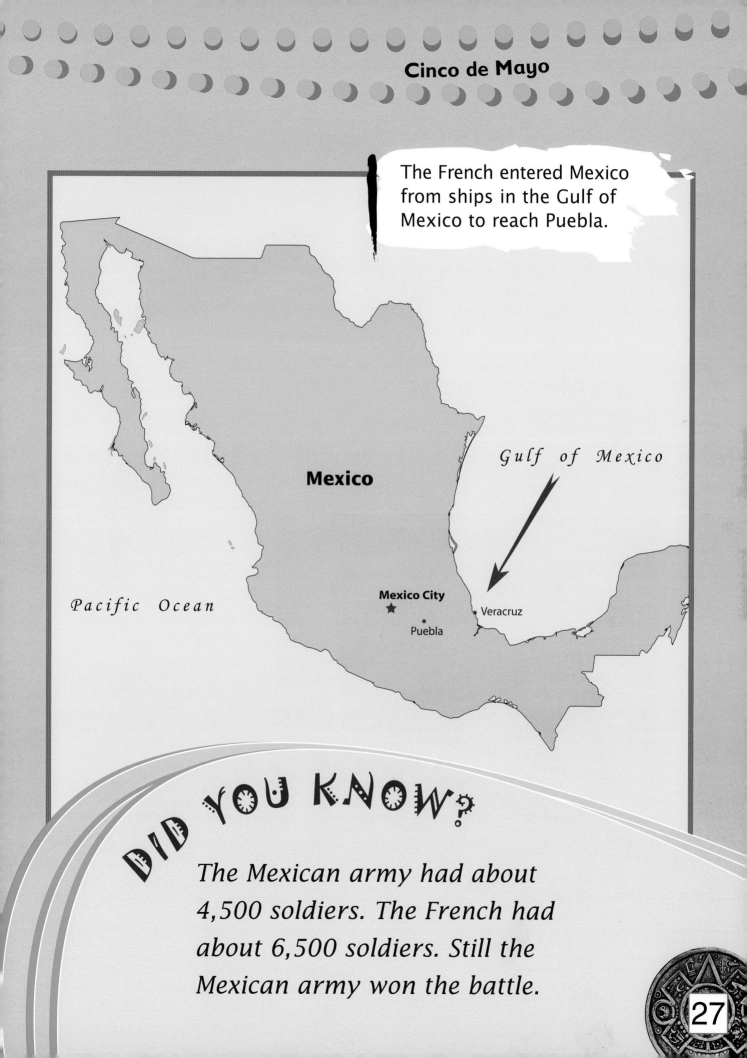

The French entered Mexico from ships in the Gulf of Mexico to reach Puebla.

Mexico

Gulf of Mexico

Pacific Ocean

Mexico City
★

Puebla

Veracruz

DID YOU KNOW?

The Mexican army had about 4,500 soldiers. The French had about 6,500 soldiers. Still the Mexican army won the battle.

27

Mexican Art

Cinco de Mayo fiestas are very colorful, creative events! These pages show some of the works of art you might see at a *Cinco de Mayo fiesta.*

- Mexican artists make *alebrijes*, or wood carvings. *Alebrijes* are often sold at *Cinco de Mayo* street fairs.

- Mexican artists weave **serapes**. A *serape* is a blanket or shawl with brightly colored designs.

DID YOU KNOW?

Papel picado *is a Mexican art form of cutting paper into patterns. You can see colorful banners or paper strips with cut patterns hanging during* Cinco de Mayo.

Mexican artists also make colorful paper flowers. The flowers are used to decorate during many holidays including *Cinco de Mayo.*

29

Viva Mexico!

The *fiesta* doesn't end when the sun sets. Fireworks color the sky late into the night of *Cinco de Mayo*.

There is much to celebrate about Mexico—from food to art to its wonderful people. And that's just what we do on *Cinco de Mayo*. Best of all, we have a good time doing it! *Fiesta*!

● Many families enjoy dining out at Mexican restaurants. Some restaurants even have *Mariachi* bands that play for you while you eat!

DID YOU KNOW?

Today, there are more Cinco de Mayo fiestas *in the United States than there are in Mexico!*

Glossary

charro A traditional costume worn by men and boys

Cinco de Mayo May 5th in Spanish

fiesta Party

Jaribe Tapatio the Hat Dance

Mariachi A band that plays traditional Mexican music

Mole Poblano The national dish of Mexico, a sauce made with spices and chocolate

piñata A decorated container filled with candy that kids break open with a stick

serape A woven blanket worn as a shawl

sombrero A wide-brimmed traditional Mexican hat

Index

art 28-29, 31

battle 6, 7, 24, 25, 26, 27

Chihuahuas 23

costumes 14-15

dancing 5, 10, 14, 15, 16, 17, 20-21, 22

Diaz, Porfirio 6

fiestas 5, 8, 12, 14, 16, 22, 24, 28, 30, 31

food 5, 10, 12-13, 14, 25, 31

games 8, 11, 20, 22

Jaribe Tapatio 20, 21

Mariachi bands 16, 17, 31

music 5, 10, 16-17, 18, 21, 22, 25

parades 18-19, 22, 23, 24

Penon 25

piñatas 8-9, 22

Puebla 24, 26, 27

serapes 28

sombreros 15

street fairs 10-11, 16, 28

Printed in the U.S.A.